Leaves From My Tree Of Life

Yvette Jaks

BALBOA.PRESS
A DIVISION OF HAY HOUSE

Copyright © 2024 Yvette Jaks.

All rights reserved. No part of this book may be used or reproduced by any means, graphic, electronic, or mechanical, including photocopying, recording, taping or by any information storage retrieval system without the written permission of the author except in the case of brief quotations embodied in critical articles and reviews.

Balboa Press books may be ordered through booksellers or by contacting:

Balboa Press
A Division of Hay House
1663 Liberty Drive
Bloomington, IN 47403
www.balboapress.com
844-682-1282

Because of the dynamic nature of the Internet, any web addresses or links contained in this book may have changed since publication and may no longer be valid. The views expressed in this work are solely those of the author and do not necessarily reflect the views of the publisher, and the publisher hereby disclaims any responsibility for them.

The author of this book does not dispense medical advice or prescribe the use of any technique as a form of treatment for physical, emotional, or medical problems without the advice of a physician, either directly or indirectly. The intent of the author is only to offer information of a general nature to help you in your quest for emotional and spiritual well-being. In the event you use any of the information in this book for yourself, which is your constitutional right, the author and the publisher assume no responsibility for your actions.

Any people depicted in stock imagery provided by Getty Images are models, and such images are being used for illustrative purposes only. Certain stock imagery © Getty Images.

Print information available on the last page.

ISBN: 979-8-7652-5183-6 (sc)
ISBN: 979-8-7652-5182-9 (e)

Library of Congress Control Number: 2024908539

Balboa Press rev. date: 04/30/2024

Contents

Dedication ix

Spring

Spring...A Way of Life 1
Good & Bad 3
My Shooting Star 5
Concierto 7
Love Blanket 9
A Child's Pleas 11
Blossom 13
A Puppet No More 15
Relinquish 17
Dysfunction 19

Summer

Attitude 23
Story of Joy 25
Bubble 27
Frend 29
Faith 31
Remember Not to Forget 33
What a Difference a Day Makes 35
A Tad Too Much 37
Whenever 39
Two Become One 41

Autumn

A Thought...45
Artwork...47
Driftwood 49
Destination..51
Fate..53
Foundation 55
Invisible Cord..57
Smiling Heart 59
Investment..61

Winter

Multi-Colored Waterfall 65
Roller Coasters 67
The Non-Material...69
The Puzzle 71
One..73
Father 75
Perspective...77
L-O-V-E 79
Job Search..81
Bricks of Life..83

Dedication

To my brothers!

Maurice for his never-ending mission to protect me through life.

Daniel for his ability to run circles around his siblings with his accomplishments, hence fueling the fire for this book.

Finally, to my partner Richard for his honest opinions and most importantly his reciprocity of unconditional love.

To quote my nephew Tre I will send this sentiment tied to my birthday 8/31.

8 letters, 3 words and 1 sentiment ~ I love you!

Paige ~ Happy 41st!
Ah to be 41 again.
♡ Yvette
2025

Enjoy Hygge этот!
Ah to be 41 again.
♡ Ryann
2025

Spring

Spring...A Way of Life	1991
Good & Bad	1994
My Shooting Star	1998
Concierto	2002
Love Blanket	2007
A Child's Pleas	2009
Blossom	2011
A Puppet No More	2012
Relinquish	2013
Dysfunction	2020

Spring...A Way of Life

Spring arrives and your surroundings begin to blossom.
At each turn of your head you are awakened by the presence of life.
Until now everything around you lay dormant in the winter snow.

Summer brings with it a heat that rises from the pavement like passion in the night.
The lushness of nature keeps you alert and, on your toes, but best of all you are lulled by the spacious starry sky.

Autumn begins to surface its beauty through color.
Every facet of the environment glistens in vivid reds, oranges and gold.
Without notice, a new layer of clothing is added.
Is this to retain the heat of summer or to keep out the cold of winter?

Winter snow has taken the place of the warm autumn rain.
The stark reality of your resistance to the elements is a struggle as each day passes. Why must winter come?

But as you gaze from a window, warmed by your thoughts you realize there is beauty even in this season.

Allow the warmth of your thoughts to melt away the cold of winter and revive the blossoming of Spring!

yj ~ 1991

Good & Bad

A childhood comes and goes, and the outcome produces an adult.

The environment in which a child is raised provides the elements that mold the character traits they possess as an adult.

The values, morals and ethics that are presented to a child formulate their personality.

Most of us exercise the ability to remember the good and forget the bad.

As a child we try so hard to be mature and act like an adult but how many of us allow the child to surface now that we are older.

These moments can be as numerous as one allows.

Recalling a nursery rhyme, squatting to play a game of jacks, or simply blowing bubbles from a wand.

Licking a lollipop, visiting an arcade, or indulging in a sweetened cereal that we once ate.

How often we wondered how different life would have been had we been born in a different place or time.

A childhood is best measured by the good memories which we so easily allow to surface, but how unbalanced life would be if we never referenced the remaining experiences which we have cataloged so carefully.

yj ~ 1994

My Shooting Star

You have come into my life for just a brief moment and in that short time you have attached yourself to my heart.

As a shoulder to cry on, you were strength. As an appreciative recipient of my humor, you were laughter. As a listener, you were attentive. As a friend you excelled.

The purpose for our connection will someday become apparent, but for now just go knowing that you will be remembered for your strength, your laughter, your sensitivity and most of all for your undaunting ability to make me feel special.

yj ~ 1998

Concierto

The heart is an instrument that plays a strong first string in most of our actions.

The consequence of these actions, at times, produces a piece so melodious that even Beethoven would be impressed.

Yet there are times when question marks may fill the bars of notes, creating a skip in the harmony of the finished product.

We must learn to allow our hearts the freedom to play its beat. Although at times it may not be rhythmic, the music it plays may be just the bar needed to complete a concierto at a later date.

yj ~ 2002

Love Blanket

Love ~ so simply written with four letters but yet so complex.

Love can bring a web of emotions to the surface and yet retain some deep down in our souls for safekeeping.

The feelings that love brings are euphoric and can elicit pangs of hunger for we can not eat, but yet they can nourish and fill our hearts to the brim with contentment.

The touch of a lover can raise the fine hairs on our outer layer but can also create a fire that burns way down to the core of our being.

The images of time spent together are cataloged in our memory bank to be selectively referenced at our own will and will occupy our empty moments for an eternity.

But even when the relationship comes to an end the thoughts of our shared love remain like a blanket that can be used at our discretion to warm us.

yj ~ 2007

A Child's Pleas

Please protect me as I trust everything and everyone.

Please discipline me through stern guidance, but with a loving heart.

Please nurture me whether boy or girl, as love does not know gender.

Please feed me as I can not distinguish between food and toys.

Please teach me right from wrong so that I too can judge good character.

Please treat me with respect so that I may build a strong self-esteem.

Please clothe me so that I may weather cold and hot.

Please care for me when I am sick and one day I may return the favor.

Please show me positive ways so that I will become a positive thinker.

Please shower me with good parenting so that childhood memories are golden.

Please love me so that I may learn to love as well.

yj ~ 2009

Blossom

Friendship, like a flower, grows from a seed.

We will call that seed introduction.

As a flower is nourished by the elements ~ soil sun and water, so is the enrichment that evolves from a friendship ~ as we shower it with love, respect, and kindness.

The awesome feeling elicited when viewing a garden in full bloom parallels the moments in life that we share with a true friend.

So, with that said, I just wanted you to know that as a friend you flourish, as a friend you shine but most importantly as my friend and like a flower, you have made me blossom.

yj ~ 2011

A Puppet No More

We wish, we dream, we try regardless of the odds.

Life begins with rituals that are orchestrated by those that brought us into the world.

We are puppets in their attempt at parenting and the molding of the creatures they have created.

We live our lives in observance of how others are treated and sometimes even wish that we were the creation of other puppeteers, but we must learn to survive in the world that fate has bestowed upon us.

We reach adulthood and the teachings of the puppeteers begin to impact the decisions that we make each day.

Unfortunately, we allow the puppet strings to show on occasion. The many times that we were chastised and made to believe that we weren't capable and that no matter how hard we wished or dreamed or tried, all others would be more powerful than us, have left a mark.

We attempt to deal with life as it unravels before us.

We feign confidence as we contend with those mal intended that cross our paths and to whom we have unintentionally given permission to surface our weaknesses.

This happens when shifts created by bad mortar in our foundation's bricks allow us to stumble.

We must overcome these challenges and sever the invisible puppet strings that we have allowed to surface and make visible for manipulation.

We must proceed with images of courage, strength and fortitude and not permit the wanna-be puppeteers that we have allowed into our lives to perpetrate the negatives.

No longer a puppet, no longer directed by a puppeteer we must wish and dream and try to make life what we want it to be…a life without strings.

yj ~ 2012

Relinquish

A child will follow the process called life and will become an adult, but it will not matter to his mother as to her he will always be her child.

Through nurturing and love she prepares him for life's trials and tribulations in hopes that this will be enough to keep him safe and sound throughout the process.

She provides shelter, education, and motherly advice. She is there to catch him most times when he stumbles and if not caresses him after the falls.

She admires the man that he has become and continues to remind herself of this fact, but she is unable to relinquish the vow of responsibility she took at conception.

Life will bring many challenges to this child and most of them he will conquer thanks to the love that has been provided. But their life consists of many paths and most of them he will travel alone.

The consequences of his choices she won't be able to control so she must learn to relinquish the intent to assist as the fate of their outcome can only be determined by a higher being.

yj ~ 2013

Dysfunction

When raised by a dictator, no matter what you did it was never good enough.

It seemed the harder you tried, the more you displeased them.

When raised by a dictator, you had to please at all costs, so unfortunately you spend the rest of your life trying to please others.

Now whenever a situation even appears to resemble the experiences you had as a child, you lash out and get defensive.

The battle is just a fight against the failures you were made to believe were yours when you should have never taken ownership of them, as they did not belong to you.

When the defensive behavior surfaces your rational mind knows that you are only lashing out at the past and not the present, but unfortunately the reaction simply creates a poor image of who you really are to the receiver.

Resolution can be attained without the defensive response, but God is it difficult to check those feelings, as the learned behavior was to stifle them as a child when you couldn't defend yourself.

Most are not privy to what feeds the learned defense mechanisms that are triggered by the fortification you built to defend your character now as an adult.

What makes you react irrationally today is sadly that there was no one there to teach you how to diffuse the dysfunctional then.

yj ~ 2020

Summer

Attitude	1995
Story of Joy	1995
Bubble	1998
Frend	1999
Faith	2000
Remember Not to Forget	2001
What a Difference a Day Makes	2012
A Tad Too Much	2012
Whenever	2013
Two Become One	2018

Attitude

Attitude, it's all about attitude.

Professional, positive, energetic, negative, immature, or maybe sometimes even down-right nasty.

The attitude you apply in a situation will with no doubt ascertain the outcome.

It is easy to blame life's problems on circumstance or even fate but consider the approach and your attitude will set the foundation to positive resolutions.

Thinking "attitude" before you act will most assuredly make your contribution to life's experiences more pleasant and productive.

yj ~ 1995

Story of Joy

Sharing can be a wonderful experience. Telling the world liberates you and magnifies the special circumstance that brought you joy.

But the most insignificant detail can cause you harm if its delivery is out of context.

Evaluate the person you choose to call a friend and with whom you share.

A friend should be a trusted confidant, but will your secrets be compromised if your relationship is interrupted by a misunderstanding?

So, choose carefully with whom you share. Your story should be as close to real life as possible. Not that you should live with distrust in your heart, but a pause in your excitement can ensure your story remains one of joy.

yj ~ 1995

Bubble

I can't explain this void within me.

It is deeper than a well with no water.

It has depth beyond the ocean floor at its deepest point.

It is a very empty place that I find to be extremely lonely.

The feelings I have cannot be defined.

For example, I feel lost but yet I never wandered.

I feel unattached yet I never let go.

But most of all, I feel alone yet I am surrounded by many.

What "the rest" is comprised of I have no earthly idea, but I do know that I must learn all the virtues that will assist me in the attainment of this level of serenity within myself.

I must burst this bubble and learn to accept life without containment.

yj ~ 1998

Frend

To define the word friend is complex. But if we look at the spelling, we find that the simplicity of the task is quite clear.

The "F" should represent…faithful.

The "R" should represent…responsible.

The "E" should represent…enriching.

The "N" should represent…nurturing.

And finally

The "D" should represent…dependable.

I know it appears that I have misspelled the word friend above, but you see, simply spoken the "I" in Friend is silent. So, to me that represents that there is no "I" in friend, only the thought of us.

yj ~ 1999

Faith

Yesterday security was a given, financial, personal, and emotional. The resources were on a stable plain.

Blessings I receive are continuous and for those I thank God, but why am I never content?

Health, employment and friends are bountiful and for those I thank God, buy why am I always questioning?

Material possessions abound and for those I thank God, but why am I always seeking more?

Patience, contentment and peace are learned traits and I continue to educate myself. For these abilities and for everything else I pray to God. May he provide me with the strength to appreciate and to exercise faith.

yj ~ 2000

Remember Not to Forget

As you take that stride towards becoming a man don't forget all that you have learned as a child.

The lessons were not all written nor bound in a book, but neither is life.

Don't forget…the memories that will always bring tears of laughter.

Don't forget…the love that abounded regardless of the hardships.

Don't forget…your loved ones because they will always be your touchstones.

Don't forget…the friends you made, their many ways and special attributes.

Don't forget…the lessons that you have learned even those that did not require a teacher.

Remember as you take these steps into the adult world that all decisions you make should be yours. The mistakes you make, the challenges you will encounter and the obstacles that you will overcome will all be a part of life.

Marry these with the achievements you will attain, the jobs that you will hold and the people that you will meet, and these will be "your" life.

So, the key to these words of wisdom is, just remember not to forget.

yj ~ 2001

What a Difference a Day Makes

I learn something new each day, but when life presents me with new challenges that require knowledge I have yet to acquire, it can be overwhelming.

I allow myself to be moved to tears because I sometimes expect more of myself than is humanly possible.

I am given instructions, but the fear of the unknown makes me question my every step.

But as a new day comes what brought me frustration the day before becomes less stressful and I approach it with a new sense of confidence.

The reason for this new feeling is that I have made every attempt to overcome the challenges and realized that even if a mistake is made, I will have the sense to recognize it and adjust accordingly!

It is refreshing to conquer new tasks, but still bothersome that I allow the learning process to consume me and that I don't afford myself the same patience that I would give to another, if I were the teacher and not the student.

I will further task myself not only to learn the functions that I have been assigned, but to acquire the fortitude to learn patience and put down the beating stick that we with high standards keep within reach when the assessment is of ourselves.

This all said, I will conquer all the challenges put before me that will make me more valuable to my peers and ultimately teach me that I am blessed with the capacity to learn.

yj ~ 2012

A Tad Too Much

Perhaps I allow my attention to be consumed by the tube as most Americans do, a tad too much.

Perhaps I allow my mouth to share what my heart can no longer hold, a tad too much.

Perhaps I allow my friends to take liberty with my time, a tad too much.

Perhaps I allow my work stress to deprive me of much needed rest, a tad too much.

Perhaps I allow my downtime to be accompanied by wine, a tad too much.

Perhaps I allow my inability to prepare culinary delights to keep me out of the kitchen, a tad too much.

But as I sit here typing I realize that perhaps I allow myself these things that appear as inadequacies to others because they lend themselves to who I have become. To relinquish them would be a tad too much.

yj ~ 2012

Whenever

I want to be there for you, whenever you feel in need.

I want to be the one you turn to, whenever you feel in need.

I want to help you reach resolution to your problems, whenever you feel in need.

I want to know you trust me, whenever you feel in need.

I want to offer solace, whenever you feel in need.

I want to offer you a warm hug, whenever you feel in need.

I want to warm your heart and fill all voids, whenever you feel in need.

I want to love you more than all the rest, whenever you feel in need.

yj ~ 2013

Two Become One

One day you walk alone and wonder what tomorrow will bring.

As you engage in life and surround yourself with friends and family you wonder if that special someone will come to complete your life.

Then that moment arrives, and it catches you completely by surprise. The special words he speaks, his acts of kindness, his heart of gold and his special like for you are enough to take your breath away.

All these years you have addressed your life with I's & Me's and Mine and now you find yourself speaking in a different dialect that includes the words Him, & He & Us.

The day arrives when he finally realizes that his life without you is incomplete and that is when he asks for your hand in marriage. You will embark on that voyage called love and will promise to weather all the sunny days and the stormy ones together ~ forever.

You will continue to engage in life, but now you will add this special person that has chosen you, to your family.

Go forward with your destiny and share your love, as today the two of you become one!

yjaks ~ 2018

Autumn

A Thought	1993
Artwork	1994
Driftwood	1995
Destination	1998
Fate	2001
Foundation	2011
Invisible Cord	2012
Consume Properly	2013
Smiling Heart	2013
Investment	2016

A Thought...

A thought can be worth money – but usually no more than a penny.

A thought escapes you – but returns at the most uncanny moment.

A thought expressed with sincerity can be emotionally moving.

A thought can be viewed as innovative, if heard by the right audience.

A thought can be offered to you with an unlimited amount of time for consideration.

A thought can be telepathic.

A thought can provoke a smile but can also bring a tear to one's eye.

A thought can be evil but also be perceived as fun by the receiver.

A thought can cross the mind but be intended to cross a great distance.

A thought can linger like the taste of a fine wine on your pallet.

A thought can be held like a flight pattern in a Blue Angels formation.

A thought can also be just that…a thought!

yj ~ 1993

Artwork

Childhood comes and goes and before the blink of an eye our lives as adults begin.

We are separated from loved ones, with the promise of keeping in touch. Our thoughts are interrupted frequently with memories that allow us to visit with them shortly, but the ability to share our new lives and embrace only happen every so often.

When we meet, we discuss our past and make attempts to relate on what we thought were the same memories but quickly we come to the realization that although our lives were painted by the same artists, the artwork was the result of a variety of inspirations.

As our paths meet once again, I appreciate the work of art before me and I take the time to memorize each brushstroke. I realize that I must do this because as our lives take a new path once again and we separate, I will cherish the new appreciation I have reached on this viewing.

Little brother, you're a fine work of art and I will always appreciate your similarities to ME but will enjoy the different brush strokes that define YOU.

yj ~ 1994

Driftwood

Special places that we find on our travels can offer a serenity or simply an escape from reality at times when we are challenged.

A corner of the world that regardless of how long the day was or how difficult the people were that crossed our path, would offer you an unwinding effect not possible anywhere else.

Having traveled from East to West and back again, and although the views offer the same elements, water, sun and a horizon, I have never encountered so special a place as my well-preserved piece of driftwood precariously set on an approachable cliff in San Francisco.

How I long for that spot as I learn to deal with the realities of life on the East Coast. As time passes, I find myself realizing that my special place did not only offer a moments pleasure, but continues to offer me peace of mind and lasting memories.

Where would we be without the ability to remember?

yj ~ 1995

Destination

The places we travel to are based on decisions we make either spontaneously or by establishing a well-defined plan.

The destination is important at the time of planning but upon arrival the outcome of our trip is measured by many variables and possibilities.

We discuss the different options that we can take on our approach to the visit be it casual, formal or carefree.

But once in place our plans may deviate based on decisions made by the host, the mood, the environment, or any other number of distractors.

It is best to approach the plan with no predetermined angle then life will consist of fewer disappointments.

yj ~ 1998

Fate

As a young girl I played with dolls as my thoughts revolved around being a mommy.

As I developed it became clear that I would never bear a child of my own. The emotion of this truth enveloped me in a trance of inadequacies and feelings of insecurity.

I came to accept my fate, although not without questioning the spiritual and medical arenas with Whys.

Many tears have been spilled over the years as the subject was broached, but thankfully the void has been filled with the love I have shared with nieces, nephews and children of friends held dear.

yj ~ 2001

Foundation

The foundation of our strength and fortitude as an individual is said to develop in the first few years of our existence.

The person that we become is comprised of many of life's experiences, but the key apprentice that forms our person and who we become is our mother.

Her maternal instincts provide for nurturing, patience, and a showering of her learned lessons in life, as she makes every attempt to sift out the mistakes and harmful ones with care.

These gifts are essential bricks in our foundation. The mortar dries as she protects it from the elements with an invisible cloak called love.

We develop from an innocent, carefree infant to a strong and fearless child in the playground of life.

As we grow up and become independent individuals, we must remember not to lose sight of those essential bricks that make us who we are and we must give thanks to our apprentice we affectionately call mother before she is gone and our words fall on deaf ears.

yj ~ 2011

Invisible Cord

Mothers give us life. The cord of birth that attached us during her pregnancy remains an invisible but binding force throughout their lives and ours.

Mothers make decisions for us and at the time they are their best attempts although we may disagree.

Later in life as we reminisce, we try to erase the memory of our childish pouting and repent our outbursts of disagreement for those things we couldn't understand at the time.

As a mother ages we catch glimpses of the pride upon her face as she gazes upon us and gleams at what she has created. If her love is reciprocated her pride increases ten-fold.

So, give to her relentlessly, as the inevitable will come and one day regrettably all that will remain of her will be the memories of moments shared.

If you have lived with appreciation of her in your heart, the now invisible cord of birth will channel her love for you and keep the timeless memories alive.

These memories will surface whenever she crosses your mind and trust that they will come to exceed the value of any worldly possession.

yj ~ 2012

Smiling Heart

No one can make us feel good or bad if we are in control of our own emotions.

But a consistent pattern of vibes that are not positive can lead to a negative existence so we can't help but feel their influence.

Energy that does not perpetrate happiness is a waste of time. Your heart should smile even if the circumstances in your life attempt to consume you.

Life is a constant battle of survival. The two areas of our lives that we place the most energy into, our careers and our relationships, can bring us escalating moments of enrichment and reward, but they can also generate moments of question and anxiety.

We must rise above these situations that create feelings of ineptitude or sadness because on the stage of life our performance should not be directed to entertain other's desires, but to surface with feeling the person that we intend to portray.

By choosing our audience carefully and selecting only those that will see the light of our spirit, we will fill our souls with an aura of fulfillment.

When shared this desire and passion will radiate like a beam of sunshine and allow us to possess a smiling heart.

yj ~ 2013

Investment

We meet a stranger and if our initial assessment deems them worthy of our time, we invest in them.

We invest of ourselves and give of our energy.

When we find a common thread, we begin to establish a bond, one that allows us to share from within.

We begin to trust this stranger that we are starting to consider a friend and hope they have our best interest at heart.

But as time moves on, we begin to formulate an assessment of the association and we realize that although we may have things in common, this person is still an individual with their own opinions, their own experiences and therefore their own perceptions and interpretations of life.

At this point we must assess how this stranger measures up. Does this measure compute when using our life's equation of good versus bad?

If the sum is favorable, then we move forward but if the balance is off kilter, we must prepare to move our investment to a more lucrative platform or lessen the amount of our investment.

yj ~ 2016

Winter

Multi-Colored Waterfall	1993
Roller Coasters	1993
The Non-Material	1994
The Puzzle	1994
One	1995
Father	1997
Perspective	1998
L-O-V-E	2002
Job Search	2008
Bricks of Life	2017

Multi-Colored Waterfall

A tree's branches bare during one season of its life can grow scented petals or simply bud into its prime leaf formation of green.

The multifaceted purposes in its perennial stages of life begin.

It can serve as a romantic foreground for a couple feigning interest in a well-prepared picnic, or it can provide the perfect hiding place for a child playing an innocent game of hide and seek.

The lushness of its leaves blocks the view of the horizon and creates a mystery for what lies in its path.

For those seeking shelter from a hot afternoon sun, languishing in the shade cast by the tree is heaven.

The journey of the tree's life serves as a camouflaging of its aging process.

The leaves, once green, burst into shades that surpass even the spectrum of colors found on an artist's palette.

Once the change occurs, the leaves remain attached for only a short-lived moment to the branches that once bore them.

A rose you must stop and smell – as the metaphor was written, but the delightful experience of color, elicited by a tree does not escape any passerby.

The fervor that once fed the tree in its growth now fades slowly. Idly standing by, awed by its final act, we observe the multi-colored waterfall.

yj ~ 1993

Roller Coasters

Life is full of nice surprises.

It pours rain one day to nourish our surroundings, then the next day the sun shines and there's a crispness to the air that lets you know you are alive.

It's wonderful to be alive! There's a positive air to what lies ahead. The holidays, new friends, and the span of new plains to be discovered.

The year approaches an end, but the prospects of the new year are full of hope. This year has brought many changes to my life, most were interesting, and some proved challenging, bringing with them a roller coaster of emotions.

The good news is that I love roller coasters, so bring on the new year!

yj ~ 1993

The Non-Material

Keep the flowers.
Keep the candy.
Keep it all.

Give me love.
Give me attention
and shower me with YOU and I'm happy.

The flowers die.
The candy is fattening.
But the non-material lasts forever and
enriches me in the best of ways.

                                                       yj ~ 1994

The Puzzle

Life can be like a puzzle. One day all the pieces are placed in a stir within the constraints of a well measured box. Undisturbed they simply represent a collection of pieces that when strategically placed have the potential for a work of art.

As you uncover the box and consider the task at hand, a puzzle can be overwhelming. But as you set your concentration to one piece at a time and the puzzle begins to come together, you become focused.

Glancing at the box you see the finished product and refer to the model quite often, but the beauty of the picture you realize requires patience, commitment, and a desire you may not be prepared for at that chosen moment.

As you lose your determination you decide to set the unfinished puzzle aside and place emphasis on a different task. As the days pass the desire to return to the puzzle slowly returns.

The puzzle's completion hinges on many variables. These variables can be perceived as obstacles, or they can be positive and inspirational, leading you to the completion of the task at hand. Your chosen perception will control the destiny of your puzzle.

As you selectively pick up the pieces of your puzzle, think masterfully of the final product.

yj ~ 1994

One

Intimacy brings forth a bonding of our inner strengths and makes us one.

Together we can overcome our weaknesses and endure all that we believe is not worth our energy.

Let us always bond and keep the magical powers alive that allow us positive thoughts and the ability to see beyond the obstacles.

yj ~ 1995

Father

A father is a provider.
A father is strength.
A father is a mentor.
A father is a friend.

If we remember all the good times and smile at all the rest, the pleasant memories of our fathers will always keep us blessed.

yj ~ 1997

Perspective

Discoveries are made on a frequent basis in life. The reality of their content can be scientific, emotional, amazing, or merely the surfacing of a small unknown.

Unraveling the character of a new acquaintance, challenging skills you weren't aware you could master, or finding that ants have taken over your favorite flowerpots, are just a few examples of our daily discoveries.

These discoveries can be insignificant, or they can make a visual difference in your life. The depth that you allow these actions can determine their impact on the formation of your thought process.

The acquaintance you have made can be allowed to climb the rungs of the friendship ladder, the one that takes them from acquaintance to friend, to good friend, to confidant, or they may simply remain just that, an acquaintance.

The skills you have mastered can define a completely new niche for your standing in the corporate world or simply be added to your already long list of strengths and qualities.

Finally, the ants you discovered in your flowerpots can be left alone to build the ant hill of their dreams, or you easily spray them and sweep them away.

A balanced perspective on your discoveries will help you determine peace of mind and ultimately your achieved level of happiness in life.

Keep things in perspective.

yj ~ 1998

L-O-V-E

L is for larceny, the crime you committed when you stole my heart.

O is for orchestrate, which is what I tend to do in life which can sometimes drive others crazy.

V is for Valentine's Day, the holiday that should be celebrated 365 days of the year.

and finally, the

E is for extraordinary, the word that should define all relationships and one that I will strive to define ours.

yj ~ 2002

Job Search

Believe that you are the best at everything to which you apply.

Believe that the internet is making a personal connection between you and the decision maker.

Believe that your resume will shine above the rest.

Believe that the position to which you have applied does not already belong to someone on board.

Believe that the pay will be commensurate with your skills.

Believe that although you are over-qualified, they will still feel your passion for the job at hand.

Believe that although you have not been selected for the last 3 positions to which you have applied that they were just not meant to be.

Believe that the right job is out there and will soon land at your feet.

But most importantly always…

Believe in yourself.

yj ~ 2008

Bricks of Life

Love is the act that conceives a child. Two people share a moment that will change their lives forever and create the beginning of another.

It is vital to remember the act of love that brought this miracle to life, so that loving thoughts will instill the strength required for your new responsibility.

Love should be the key ingredient in making this child your priority.

If you consider this creation a wall building endeavor and liberally apply mortar to each brick, then you will have peace of mind in its architectural integrity.

There will be many bricks added throughout the child's life… nurturing, commitment, determination, encouragement and an endless number of others because keeping them out of harms way and wanting for nothing are just some of the instinctual priorities.

So, keep the mortar (love) tray at hand's reach and reapply as needed, as this will ensure the integrity of your wall building project and when challenged withstand the test of time…a lifetime.

yj ~ 2017